ESSENTIAL KNOTS

ANDREW ADAMIDES

This edition published in 2025 by Arcturus Publishing Limited
26/27 Bickels Yard, 151–153 Bermondsey Street,
London SE1 3HA

AD008670UK

Printed in China

CONTENTS

INTRODUCTION

This book has been divided into seven main sections, each focusing on one of the different categories of knot. These seven sections are as follows: the first concerns bends, the second binding knots, the third hitches, the fourth loops, the fifth slip knots, the sixth splices and the seventh stopper knots.

The eighth section is dedicated to trick and fancy knots – the knots featured can of course fall into one of the previous seven sections, but have been highlighted in this chapter because they have unique characteristics that make them stand out from the crowd. These characteristics vary; some can simply be tied in an unusually rapid way, some untie in a distinctive manner. Others are simply very decorative or have uncommon applications.

Each knot type is used for different applications, and each is defined in the individual section introductions. The uses, strengths and weaknesses of each individual knot are featured. You will find illustrated step-by-step instructions for each knot on the cards. Each individual entry's difficulty level is illustrated through a star rating system, where knots rated with just one star are the easiest, and those with four stars are the hardest.

On reading the knot descriptions and instructions, the novice knot tyer will no doubt notice quickly that there are certain words and terms related to knotting which they may not previously have come across.

The Glossary section provides definitions for all the knotting terms used within the book. We also provide similar definitions for some basic tools used in knotting and rope work, and an overview of the different types of rope and line.

While every effort has been taken to ensure the accuracy of the knot illustrations and descriptions featured in this book, it is advised that if you plan to use the knots while in a potentially hazardous or dangerous situation, that you should check with a qualified practitioner of knot tying before using the particular knot.

THE HISTORY OF KNOTS AND ROPE

Ever since man began to use the objects, plants and creatures around him to make his life easier, he has been tying knots. Indeed, it is widely thought that the first knots were tied in Neolithic times when Neolithic Man first tied a stone to a stick, creating a tool or weapon.

Neolithic Man's immediate successors proceeded to employ knots to hold together the components used to make shelters and for creating bridges to cross territory that nature had previously made hard or impossible to traverse. And from there on, man became ever more aware of how beneficial knots could be.

Across the planet, new uses were constantly found for knots and rope as various civilizations incorporated them into their daily life. Indeed, rope was considered so important by the Ancient Egyptians, that braided and coiled rope was among the objects left in their pharaohs' tombs for use in the afterlife. Archaeologists found such lines in the tomb of Tutankhamun.

The Greeks and Romans put knots to medical use. The earliest written descriptions of knots which still exist date from the 4th century, where doctors of the age wrote of how they used a number of knots to make no fewer than 16 different varieties of slings for broken or wounded limbs. One particular knot described, now known as the Square or Reef Knot and included in this book, was also employed by weapon-makers of the time, as many swords, daggers and similar items excavated by archaeologists used the knot to hold their handles together. Many of these can now be seen in museums worldwide.

Beyond being used to manufacture items, hold things in place and join objects together, knots have been put to a wide variety of other uses throughout history. In Inca civilizations in Peru, people used string with different knots tied in it instead of writing characters down on paper. Other cultures have linked certain knots with religion, magic and even curses, with some knots tied to bring ill-fortune and others tied to ward it off.

Knots have also been used for decorative purposes throughout history, be they tied, painted or moulded. The Romans used their

form to decorate urns, while they have also appeared moulded into the decorative work of buildings throughout history. Lace-making, macramé and similar crafts have also employed knotting in the creation of fabrics all over the world. And, amazingly, humans are not the only creatures to use knotting for practical purposes – studies have shown that gorillas tie knots in order to hold together branches and vines used to make their nests. Among the knots tied by these highly intelligent creatures are Granny and Reef Knots. Similarly, some birds have been observed tying knots in stalks when building their nests.

With the discovery of knotting came the dawn of rope-making, as archaeological evidence has shown that plant fibres were used by the first knot-tyers, as was catgut, made from the gut of animals slaughtered by these early tribes. Other substances known to have been used in early rope-making include flax, leather, animal hair and papyrus hemp, which was first used in China around 2800 BCE.

As natural fibres obviously decompose over time, very few actual artifacts remain from these early eras, although some very rare pieces are held in museums. The earliest known example of actual manufactured rope is thought to date from around 17,000 BCE, when hand-twisted rope was made from plant fibres. Needless to say, this would have been extremely time-consuming. Some Ancient Egyptian writings have suggested attempts at creating very simple rope-making machines by finding ways to tie down the strands in order to make twisting them together easier.

These inscriptions have been interpreted as depicting the fibres being tied to an already-made rope, or to an object like a dowel or beam. Almost identical methods for rope-making were found in indigenous civilizations in the Americas dating back to 1000 CE. This would be some 5,000 years after the Egyptian inscriptions were made.

As for the substances used in rope-making, the Egyptians mostly employed water-reed fibres. The finished product was of great importance to their society as not only was it thought to be of use in the afterlife but it was needed to move the giant, heavy stones used to make the pyramids and other structures.

As rope-making spread across the world, new methods were sought to make its manufacture ever easier. Even the great Leonardo da Vinci designed a rope-making machine, although it never got off the drawing board. On a more practical level, the Middle Ages saw the introduction of rope walks; buildings constructed specifically for the purpose of making rope. These buildings were extremely long, and allowed long strands to be laid out flat, and then twisted together to make the rope. These ropes could be in excess of 300 yards in length, which meant that there was less need for them to be spliced together for use in the rigging of the sailing ships of the era. Rope walks could be found across Europe throughout the 13th to 18th centuries, by which time several functioning rope-making machines had been invented.

As anyone with even a passing knowledge of knotwork and rope-making will know, it is this period that saw the evolution of many of the knots still in use today. Indeed, after the Greek descriptions of the 4th century, the next written descriptions of knots date from the 18th century. This period saw more use of sailing ships than ever before, which required huge amounts of rigging in their sails, with miles of rope and numerous knots employed to hold it all together.

At this time, ship voyages took far longer than in later years and the sailors of the day had plenty of free time to while away at sea. Most were unable to either read or write, thus cutting down even further the number of leisure-time activities available to them. However, there was always a lot of rope and line on board. Using this time to tie and develop new knots became a favourite pastime among sailors, who also named the knots, resulting in some of the more unusually named knots featured in this book.

CHOOSING A KNOT

While each of the different categories of knots included here is applicable in different situations (explained in their individual sections), there are some general criteria to bear in mind when deciding on what knot should be used. Firstly, attention should be paid to the particular knot's strength. Secondly, working conditions should be considered – will the knot need to be tied quickly and easily or in a confined space: bear in mind that individual knots work better in some situations than others. Lastly, the size of the finished knot should also be assessed; if it needs to slide through an eye, hole or similar, obviously a knot that is too large or bulky cannot be used.

TOOLS

There are a number of tools which are designed to be used when knotting or undertaking rope work. The specialist tools, fids and marlinspikes, are mentioned within the text of this book and are defined in our Glossary section. However, some other common tools used include:

Mallet Mallets are made from either wood or rubber. A medium-sized mallet will be best for most rope work. Mallets are used for shaping rope or for 'bedding-down' splices.

Knife Used, obviously enough, for cutting a rope or line. A high-quality knife with a sharp blade is one of the most important parts of any rope worker's kit but, as with all sharp objects, it should be handled with the utmost care.

Needles Needles used for rope work are large and thick. They can also be used to repair sails, and specialist three-sided needles can be purchased for this, although the casual rope worker can generally make do with a large household needle.

Pliers These can be used to manipulate rope in instances where it is stiff or where it needs to be bent into a particularly acute shape, or where fingers are not strong enough.

Scissors These can be used as an alternative to a knife for cutting a rope or line. Again, they should be sharp and strong, particularly if they are going to be required to cut through thick line. And, as with knives, care should always be taken when using scissors as they can be highly dangerous when sharp.

ROPE CHOICE & CARE

Rope suitable for a particular application must always be selected with care. When using newly-purchased rope, make a note of the maker's name, the date on which the rope was produced, its average breaking load and safe working load, its weight, and the material used to make it.

Often this information can be found written on a tape embedded in the rope itself, or on the packaging. If using rope that has already been used, always take into consideration its age, condition and any wear and tear that is apparent. Before using any rope, old or new, you should check it thoroughly for any obvious defects, especially when personal safety may depend on the rope.

To ensure that rope lasts as long as possible, it is suggested that you should avoid having it run tightly over sharp edges or very rough surfaces for extended periods of time. Also, avoid stepping on it and forcing it into sharply kinked shapes. Ropes should be stored in coils, and should be dry when put away. They should also be regularly examined for dirt or corrosive substances which, if found, should be rinsed off. This also applies to salt water, which can be very damaging, especially to natural-fibre ropes.

CHAPTER ONE

BENDS

DEFINITION

A bend is a knot that attaches two lines to each other, end-to-end.

GENERAL PURPOSE AND USES

Bends are, by definition, joining knots. As such, they are used whenever it is necessary to lengthen a piece of rope, cord, string or other similar material by attaching another length to its end. Bends are also used in order to fasten two or more lines to each other in a large loop in order to create a sling or similar lifting device.

Many bends have maritime origins, having been developed for use in the rigging of various types of sails, and many of them date back several centuries – at least one is recorded as being in use as far back as the 6th century. But new variations on the classic bend knot are constantly being developed. While still used in sailing, bends today have countless applications in a wide range of activities from climbing and caving to net making.

Most bends are designed to join lines of similar diameter and material. Certain more specific types, however, can be used in situations where lines of differing diameter require joining. As with all types of knot, there are various types of bend, each with its own best use – some are better suited to consistent load-bearing, for example, while others are better in situations where the line, once tied, will be subject to strain that varies in angle and consistency, such as that exerted by a boat tied to a dock.

CHARACTERISTICS OF A BEND

Bends are generally considered to be temporary knots in that they can usually be untied and the material used to tie them re-used. That said, some are more easily untied than others, so the use of harder-to-release bends should be limited to situations in which the knot is intended as a permanent fixture (although a shroud knot or splice is generally better suited to permanent joins). As a rule of thumb, bends utilizing a thick tie line are easier to untie; those with a finer tie line tend to be more permanent.

While bends joining lengths of similar material are usually strong and stable knots, those that unite lines that differ in size, texture or flexibility can be significantly weaker – although certain types of bend are better suited to this latter use than others. In many cases, bends tying different types of material together display similar characteristics to hitches.

Although they may appear to be a viable alternative, binding knots should never be used in place of bends, as they are far more likely to slip. It should also be noted that, while some bends are stronger than others, some will cause a certain amount of wear to the lines involved – a fact that should be taken into account when deciding which type of bend to employ.

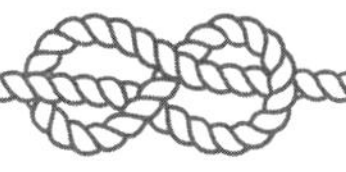

TYPES OF BENDS

SHEET BEND (CARD 1)

Quick to make and easy to untie, the Sheet Bend works well in joining lines of varying thickness or material. It is stable when placed under moderate stress, but it is not known for its strength. The knot works best with lines that are not too stiff and, if necessity calls for it to be used in conjunction with stiff lines or those that are wet or slippery, it should be made into a Double Sheet Bend for extra strength. This knot is widely employed in the construction of nets.

CARRICK BEND (CARDS 2 AND 3)

While its artistic applications are many, the Carrick Bend is most practically useful in joining together large ropes, cables or similar lines, and can also be used in uniting lines with slightly varying thicknesses. Although it has a reputation for strength, even the sturdier Carrick Bend with Ends Opposed can have an efficiency rating of as low as 65 per cent, and if the ends of the knot are not seized then the bend will 'collapse' – leaving it workable, but extremely difficult to untie. This unfortunate failing can also occur when the knot is wet or subjected to heavy stress.

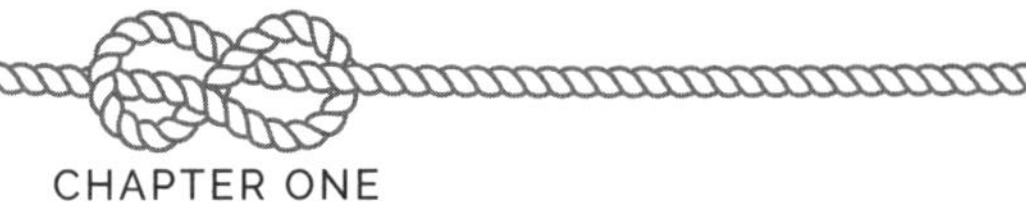

FISHERMAN'S KNOT (CARD 4)

The Fisherman's Knot is most commonly used to tie together fine line or thin pieces of rope of similar or equal diameters – a fact that makes it ideal for joining lengths of fishing line, the purpose for which it was most likely invented and from which its most popular name is derived.

When thicker lines are involved, the Fisherman's Knot becomes easier to untie; the thinner the lines being used, the greater the likelihood that they will need to be cut in order to separate them again. When tied in thin lines and pulled tight, the knot becomes extremely small and, although the knot is both strong and secure in itself, the act of tying it will considerable weaken the lines involved – a fact that should be considered before making any attempt to re-use them.

FLEMISH BEND (CARD 5)

The Flemish Bend is most widely used in climbing, a field in which it excels thanks to its strength, stability and the ease with which team leaders can check that it has been tied properly. In addition, it is also relatively easy to untie, especially when used with thicker lines, and this remains the case even after it has been subjected to considerable stress. It is unlikely to jam and causes less wear than many bends to the lines used to tie it, allowing them to be re-used with a considerable amount of confidence. The Flemish Bend works best with lines of medium thickness and can be used in conjunction with fairly slick material. The only downside is that it can be rather bulky.

HUNTER'S BEND (CARD 6)

Square in shape and extremely stable, the Hunter's Bend is used in sailing and, to a lesser extent, in climbing. Like the Flemish Bend, it is both easy to untie and very well suited to modern, synthetic ropes. It also works well with rope or line that is stiff or slippery, and with flexible line such as bungee cord. It works best when joining lines of similar or equal diameter that are not too thick.

VICE VERSA (CARD 7)

The Vice Versa is best suited to joining lines that have a slick or slippery surface, whether this is natural or due to the surrounding conditions. Thanks to its unique construction, it is also useful when working with elasticated material, making it a natural choice for joining bungee cords or modern synthetic ropes. The knot is both fairly stable and easy to undo. It is also relatively small, and as such is useful in situations where the line needs to pass through an eye or similar circular mooring.

ZEPPELIN BEND (CARD 8)

The Zeppelin Bend is known for its security and the veritable impossibility of it jamming. As such, it is ideal for use with heavy duty lines or ropes and, while there may be little call for tethering airships today, it is nevertheless perfect for use in mooring boats because of its ability to cope with heavy loads and stress, even when the latter is not constant or continuous. The knot can generally be untied fairly easily, although it may require somewhat more effort if it has been placed under stress.

CHAPTER TWO

BINDING KNOTS

DEFINITION

A Binding Knot is one tied into a line for the purpose of holding an object or objects together or in place.

GENERAL PURPOSE AND USES

Binding knots are useful in any situation where a single item needs to be held in place or a number of items bound together. As such, binding knots are used for everything from securing groups of metal poles to tying up wrapping paper on parcels and even the compression of bandages by doctors. Many such knots date back centuries, although they've been much improved upon over the years, while others are more recent creations.

Binding knots vary greatly in their strengths, and different variations are, as always, suited to different materials and applications. It should be noted, however, that it is always highly unadvisable to use binding knots in place of bends as they are neither designed for, nor suited to the same purposes, especially in potentially dangerous situations.

CHARACTERISTICS OF BINDING KNOTS

Binding knots can be divided into two distinct categories differentiated by their basic forms. In the case of the first, sometimes

referred to as the Friction Type, the line being used to tie the knot is wound round the object to be held in place several times and then passed under itself. This creates internal friction, which in turn holds the knot together. The second category, known as the Knotted Ends Type, requires the line to be wound round the objects to be tied and the ends then knotted together to secure the object.

Each category is suited to different types of application; the Friction Type is best employed when the items to be bound are of narrow diameter – in clamping a hosepipe to a tap, for example. The Knotted Ends Type works best for objects with wider diameters, such as when securing or compressing bandages to arms or legs.

Binding knots vary greatly in strength, from the very secure to the easily untied, and can be used for both semi-permanent and temporary purposes. Generally speaking, binding knots are best tied with two ends of the same piece of line, although they can also be tied using two separate pieces of similar material. They are not recommended for use with two lines that differ greatly in thickness or texture.

TYPES OF BINDING KNOTS

REEF KNOT (CARD 9)

Beside its obvious use in fastening the likes of shoelaces and belts, the Reef Knot has many other applications. It is best employed in situations where it is joining together the ends of one line to hold an object in place, and where such fastening is not intended to be permanent. It is also used often in macramé and, as mentioned earlier, for securing bandages and slings. It is also commonly used to tie rubbish bags.

Although easy to tie, the Reef Knot is not known for its strength. As such, it can be used as a general purpose binding knot, but should only be employed when it can be tied in such a way that the completed knot lies snugly against the surface of whatever it is securing. Under no circumstances should the knot be used in place of a bend, as it will give a false impression of strength before quickly unravelling. Further to this, it should never be used in a situation where reliance on it places life in the balance. This viewpoint has been endorsed by the International Guild of Knot Tyers, with some sources claiming that the failure of Reef Knots when employed in the wrong situations has been responsible for more deaths than all other knots put together.

Lastly, it should be noted that Reef Knots work best when tied using the opposite ends of either the same or similar lines; if there is any difference between the lines in terms of texture, thickness or stiffness, this will weaken the knot considerably

GRANNY KNOT (CARD 10)

The Granny Knot is, all told, pretty useless. The only time when it might actually come into its own is on those rare occasions where a knot is required that can come apart at the merest pull – although its tendency to jam makes it rather unsuitable even then. As such, we include it here more as a warning than an instruction: by understanding how it is formed, one can avoid making it accidentally and recognize when others have made it by mistake. The knot is most commonly found in poorly tied shoelaces, in which cases it almost always results in the loops of the bow coming undone and the knot itself needing to be picked apart with fingernails to much annoyance.

MILLER'S KNOT (CARD 11)

The knot's suitability for securing bags and sacks stems from the fact that it is semi-permanent, but can be loosened and tightened with relative ease and with little or no loss of strength. As such, it allows the user access to the contents of the sack and allows him or her to reseal it after more has been added or removed, with no loss of security. In addition to being used for tying off sacks, the knot is commonly used to tie hay bales and by hikers and campers securing their bags to tree branches to keep them off the ground.

BOA KNOT (CARD 12)

The Boa Knot was devised with the aim of holding together objects due to be cut through and keeping them together after this action has taken place. As such, the knot works best when used to tie together numerous long, thin objects in a cylindrical bundle – poles, for example, or sticks. The knot is strong, secure and straightforward to tie.

CONSTRICTOR KNOT (CARD 13)

The Constrictor Knot is extremely versatile – some suggest that it has more diverse uses than any other single knot – and in its various forms has been widely recognized as one of the knots that a novice should learn to tie first. Its versatility derives largely from the fact that it can be tied using almost any line, and so can be used in a wide range of situations and applications. For example, it is ideal when sealing a sack, soft bag or similar with a cord, or for attaching line to a nail or other protruding object, but it is equally at home providing temporary whipping for the end of a rope, or holding bundles of objects or other lines together.

The knot is extremely secure and easy to tie. It can be used as either a temporary or permanent knot, but should generally not be used with soft or easily damaged materials that need to retain their appearance, as it is notorious for leaving track marks.

CHAPTER THREE

HITCHES

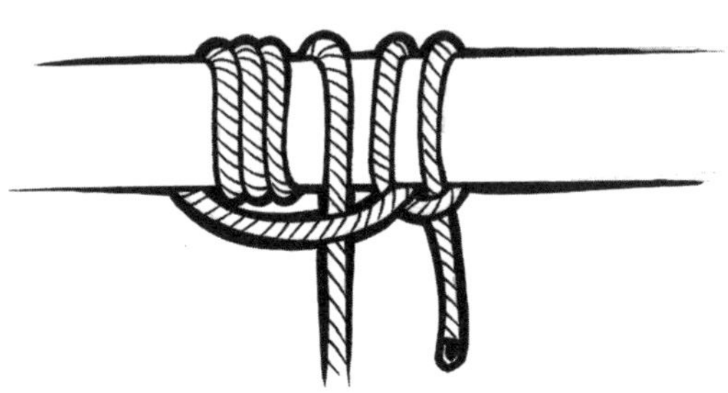

DEFINITION

Hitches are knots that fasten a line to an immovable object, such as a horizontal rail, vertical post or ring.

GENERAL PURPOSE AND USES

Hitches are exclusively used for tying lines to immovable objects. As such, their uses include the tethering of animals, the mooring of small boats and the tying of rigging or sails aboard ships. Strangely enough, lines fastened to objects using hitches are never referred to as being 'hitched', but rather 'made fast' – even in cases where the line is tied to the centre of another line or rope. Many hitches were developed on board ships, and date from a time when more sea-going craft had sails and rigging than do so today.

There are many different types of hitch, each of which will work best for different applications. Some, for example, work better under conditions in which the force exerted on the line used to tie them is at right angles to the object to which it is attached; others are better suited to applications in which the pull will be intermittent in force and its angle will vary. Further distinctions can be made between hitches that are best suited for tying to upright bollards, around rings or for tethering to horizontal beams, while some are notable for being easier to untie than others, especially when wet or in unfavourable conditions.

CHARACTERISTICS OF HITCHES

Hitches are designed to hold when force is exerted on the rope used to tie them, and can be tied in almost any material. Their strength obviously varies dramatically, but some of the most basic hitches are very weak. Most are also impermanent; while they will generally not come undone when force is exerted on the line used to tie them, they can usually be untied when the proper steps to do so are taken, although some hitches will be more difficult to unravel than others.

Interestingly, hitches can also be used to attach two lines together, but not in the same way as a bend. A hitch can be used in any instance where one line is being tied to the centre of another, at which times they differ structurally from bends in that they involve wrapping the second line around the first, rather than knotting the two together. As such, hitches should never be used in place of a bend, as they will not hold, nor should a bend be attempted in any situation where a hitch is required.

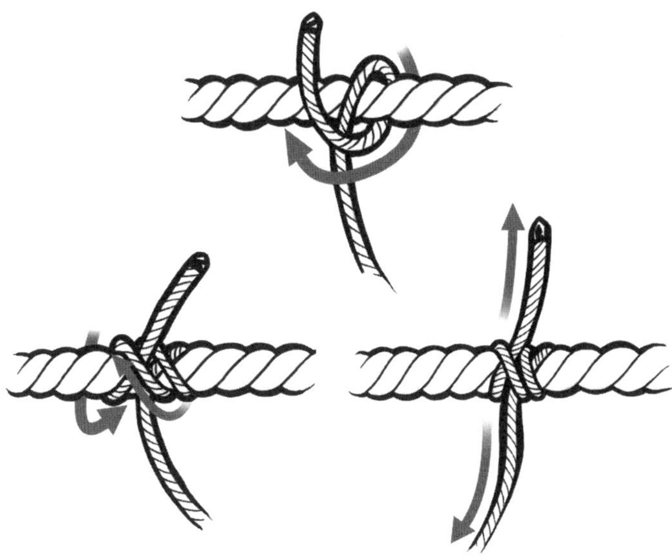

TYPES OF HITCHES

CLOVE HITCH (CARD 14)

The Clove Hitch is not strong, and its tendency to slip or jam at inopportune moments means that it should never be used in any important or life-threatening applications. It works better with lines that are thick and rugged rather than thin or slick-surfaced; on thinner, slippery lines it will come loose far more easily. To be fair, the only situations in which the Clove Hitch is of any real use are those in which equal or near-equal loads are applied to either end of the cord in which it is tied – in any other situation, it will almost certainly come loose.

HALF HITCH (CARD 15)

While easy to tie in almost any line, the Half Hitch is not particularly strong when used on its own, and has a tendency to unravel in all but the best conditions. However, it is extremely useful as a fortifying knot when applied to the working end of another hitch, and can thus either hold the other hitch in place or make its bond stronger, depending on the circumstances. The Clove Hitch is one example of a hitch that can benefit from the addition of a Half Hitch (although it can also be applied to any type of knot where there is leftover length in the working end). The Half Hitch is also a very attractive knot, and is widely used in the creation of French Whipping and in other creative pursuits. The knot can be tied as either a single knot or as Two Half Hitches, with the latter being significantly stronger.

FISHERMAN'S BEND (CARD 16)

As the sailors of the 18th century quickly found, the Fisherman's Bend is ideal for mooring smaller boats; it was also then the most popular way of fastening an anchor to a rope (hence the common variation on its name). The knot is strong to the point of being extremely difficult, if not impossible, to untie. It also has the added versatility of being usable in virtually any sort of rope or line, and capable of retaining its stability even when wet, something else that over the centuries cemented its popularity in the maritime world.

PRUSIK KNOT (CARD 17)

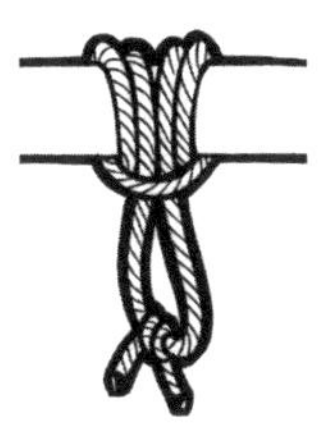

The Prusik Knot was long ago displaced from its general use in climbing by more high-tech ascender devices, although it can still be employed in an emergency for the same purpose – namely, ascending a static line – at which times the knot is tied around the rope in question and slid up in stages.

As explained above, the Prusik works well for this particular purpose because it provides a loop to grip onto and, while it can be easily slid further up the static line to which it is tied, it will not slide back down. Its use is not limited to mountaineering, however: it can also be used for climbing poles, trees or similar upright objects, and is regularly employed by rescue teams the world over.

The Prusik Knot is generally easy to get to grips with, and works well on most types of line, although obviously, if it is to be used as a safety device in any kind of potentially dangerous climbing activity, the line needs to be sturdy enough to support the climber in question

CAMEL HITCH (CARD 18)

The Camel Hitch is extremely useful in any number of situations that don't actually involve tying up a live camel. In particular, the knot is regularly employed in the sailing world thanks to the fact that it holds up well when wet and can be pulled on hard from any direction without coming loose. It is also both quick and easy to tie, and can be constructed in lines of various materials and of almost any thickness.

HIGHWAYMAN'S HITCH (CARD 19)

The Highwayman's Hitch is ideal for tying up any line that needs be released at speed, from a distance, or under conditions in which manoeuvring is difficult – hence the highwayman story. However, it is most likely that by the time the getaway came, the knot would already have capsized, so unreliable is the Highwayman's Hitch when it comes to strength and stability. As such, it isn't suitable for anything that needs to be held too securely.

ROLLING HITCH (CARD 20)

While sharing basic characteristics and strengths, the Rolling Hitch's two variant forms are best used for two entirely separate applications. The first variant should be employed when the line used to tie it is being joined to another line, and the second in cases in which it is being tied to a beam or other solid object.

The Rolling Hitch is known for its ability to withstand strain, and if tied snuggly enough it should not get any tighter under this load. However, the knot is better tied in natural-fibre ropes, as those made of modern synthetic materials will offer less grip and make the knot more likely to slip – indeed, it may be impossible to tie this knot at all with extremely slippery lines. *The Ashley Book of Knots* also suggests that while the version used for attaching two lines together is the more steadfast of the two, the second version is less likely to become twisted

TIMBER/KILLICK HITCHES (CARD 21)

The Timber Hitch's most popular application is the fastening of lines to felled logs or similar objects to help tow them to another location. The Killick Hitch has similar uses, but exerts a far harder grip, even when tied to objects with a more slippery finish. That said, both knots are strong, simple to untie and can be made in almost any type of line.

CHAPTER FOUR

LOOPS

DEFINITION

A knot made by doubling a line back on itself to create a loop and then tying the working end to the standing part.

GENERAL PURPOSE AND USES

Loops are generally used in similar instances to hitches, although they can also occasionally take the place of bends; hitches secure a line to an object (usually immovable), while bends join two lines together. A loop can be used in either of these instances, although it differs from the other two knot families in form.

Most loops have their origins in maritime usage, and many are still used in sailing to this day. They are also highly popular among mountaineers and fishermen, the former using them to provide secure foot- and handholds, the latter to attach hooks and lures to lines.

The practice of using loops in place of a bend to join ropes involves interlocking two loops; when used in place of a hitch, the loop is placed around a given object and pulled tight. Their various uses have led to many loops being considered among the most important of knots, and they are often some of the first to be taught as a result.

CHARACTERISTICS OF LOOPS

Loops fall into two distinct categories: loops in the end, where the loop is tied in the end of the line, and loops in the bight, where the loop is made in the centre of the line. On top of that, there are single, double and triple loops to contend with – and, as might be expected, single loops are the easiest to tie, although most variations are relatively straightforward to master.

While regularly serving in place of bends or hitches, loops differ in their basic structure from both of these knots. A bend is tied around an object, while a loop is first tied and then placed around the object before being drawn tight. Unlike hitches, loops can be removed from the object they have anchoring, remaining intact where a hitch would almost certainly come untied. Similarly, where a bend requires that the two lines in question be knotted together, loops allow them to be simply tied around each other, rather than to each other, and the fact that they can be loosened and slid up and down the line allows them to be adjusted and reused to secure different objects of various sizes.

TYPES OF LOOPS

OVERHAND LOOP (CARD 22)

The Overhand Loop is probably the easiest of all loops to tie, but it is not necessarily the strongest: while reasonably secure in natural fibre line, it is less stable in synthetic materials, although it can be tied in virtually any type of line. It is also one of the more difficult loops to untie from any material, especially if it has become wet or been placed under excessive strain. As previously mentioned, it is most commonly used to tie fishing hooks to lines, although it is also regularly employed to tie down loads on trucks or wagons. The Double Overhand Loop, also described below, suffers from many of the same flaws, but is slightly stronger.

BOWLINE (CARD 23)

There are numerous 'loop in the end' knots, all of them capable of being tied around a post, bollard or similar object, but the Bowline is unique among its peers thanks to its potential for being passed around the object in question prior to being tied. As such, tying two Bowlines can be a good way of joining a pair of lines together or fixing a line that has snapped – although it should be borne in mind when doing so that there are other, stronger methods for joining lines.

Primarily, the Bowline remains most frequently used on board sailing ships, where it can be employed for any purpose that requires a single loop knot. It is also a popular addition to safety harnesses, tied around the waists of sailors for support when working over the side of a vessel, or by climbers as a back-up system to their regular climbing harnesses.

Even after it has been subjected to heavy stress, the Bowline remains easy to untie – a fact greatly adding to its usefulness as a support knot – although it is remarkably strong while tied. That said,

if the load placed upon it is varied over time, or the line itself is jerked repeatedly, it can become loosened. It is easy and quick to tie, can be learned rapidly and is well suited to most types of line.

ANGLER'S LOOP (CARD 24)

The Angler's Loop is considered to be a good loop for general use in a wide variety of applications. It is simple to learn and easily tied at speed, although its tendency to jam in natural-fibre ropes led to it falling out of favour with sailors in the past – a problem largely rectified by the proliferation of modern synthetic lines.

The knot is strong and secure, although once pulled tight it is extremely difficult – if not impossible – to untie, often necessitating cutting of the line. As such, it should only be used when a permanent knot is required. It can be tied in both thick lines and in flexible cable such as bungee cords.

FIREMAN'S CHAIR KNOT (CARD 25)

This particular loop is these days most widely used to manoeuver rescue victims in emergency situations where no safety harness is available. It is a double-loop knot and, when used to move an accident victim or other person, one loop should be passed under the armpits to support the body while the other goes beneath the knees. Pulling these loops snug to the body should allow the manipulation of even unconscious people with only minimal risk or danger of falling. The knot is suitable for use with most types of line (although any being used to support a person's weight should obviously be strong), and is easily learned and quick to tie. It also benefits from being easily adjustable, allowing the person in the harness it creates to be freed from its grip rapidly when desired. Its basic structure strongly resembles that of the Handcuff Knot.

ENGLISHMAN'S LOOP (CARD 26)

The Englishman's Loop is a strong knot that works well with modern synthetic ropes and similar lines, but struggles when tied in particularly shiny surfaced material such as nylon. It once enjoyed a degree of popularity among the climbing community, but has since fallen out of favour and been replaced by knots like the Alpine Butterfly (below). Large and bulky, the Englishman's Loop is fairly easy to tie, but often difficult to untie.

ALPINE BUTTERFLY KNOT (CARD 27)

The Alpine Butterfly Knot's primary use remains in mountaineering, where it is most often employed by climbers to attach themselves to the centre of a rope. Its suitability for this purpose is derived from the fact that it retains its extraordinary strength when pulled in various directions, and can thus be trusted with a climber's suspended weight even when he or she is moving around erratically. The knot can also act as a bend for the emergency reattachment of broken rope ends. While not the easiest of knots to tie, the Alpine Butterfly does have the advantage of being suitable for almost any type of line, and easy to untie unless it has become wet.

FIGURE OF EIGHT LOOP (CARD 28)

Still widely used both in the mountains and at sea, the Figure of Eight Loop has also found applications in camping and caving. It is a fairly versatile knot in that it can be tied in the centre of a rope or in one that has been doubled over, as well as being reliable where the line is slippery. It is also easy to learn, can be tied very quickly and is famously strong and secure. On the downside, excessive pressure exerted on the rope can cause the knot to jam, making it subsequently difficult to untie, plus the Figure of Eight Loop is rather large and bulky, meaning that it won't pass through an eye or similar circlet.

CHAPTER FIVE

SLIP KNOTS

DEFINITION

Slip knots, also known as running knots, break down into two distinct categories: in the first are those knots used to fasten a line to a particular object, and which tighten when a load is placed on the end; in the second are those knots that fasten one line to the centre of another line, and which then allow the knot to slide along this line either in one direction or both directions.

GENERAL PURPOSE AND USES

The two varieties of slip knot are used in different ways. Automatically tightening knots are used in snares to trap animals, although one more day-to-day usage is the mooring of boats, particularly in conditions where the tide may rise or fall, or where the boat may be subject to currents that place irregular stress on the line, causing it to become more secure in the process. The other variety of slip knot, in which the knot can move up or down a second line to which it has been tied, is most widely used in mountaineering. Originally, these knots provided a means for climbing up ropes safely but, with the onset of modern technology, they are now mostly used as back-up safety devices.

CHARACTERISTICS OF A SLIP KNOT

Since slip knots are used to tie objects to lines or to fasten ropes together, they are also technically hitches; while every hitch is not a

slip knot, all hitches can be converted into slip knots by tying them around the standing part of their lines, and some hitches are slip knots by default. Both the Clove Hitch and Rolling Hitch, featured in the hitch section of this book, are also slip knots.

The second variety of slip knot – those that move along a rope to which the line has been attached – generally all feature a large loop, usually used to gain a foot- or handhold in climbing. As this loop does not usually go around either an object or the second rope, however, these knots are not considered members of the loop family.

TYPES OF SLIP KNOTS

SLIP KNOT (CARD 29)

The Slip Knot has a variety of diverse uses. In the countryside, it has been used widely in the creation of basic snares for catching birds, rabbits or other small creatures, while in the home it is another of the knots most often used to tie packages. In climbing, it can be used to create a tie-off point, or to attach gear to a line. While fairly secure, it should not be used in situations where it is expected to support a person's weight, as it may not be strong enough for this purpose. The knot is very easy and quick to tie and is adaptable to almost any material. It can also be rapidly unraveled by simply pulling on one end of the rope – and as such it is ideal for use in temporary applications.

RUNNING BOWLINE (CARD 30)

Needless to say, while this knot's basic structure and name may recall the standard Bowline, the fact that it is in fact a slip knot means that it is most useful under completely different circumstances. While the Bowline is used to anchor sails and the like, the Running Bowline can be utilized for a variety of purposes – as a noose to hoist large weighty sacks, for example, or in the production of animal snares. Its loop can also be lowered into deep holes or bodies of water to recover lost objects – a purpose to which it lends itself well thanks to the fact that the knot is secure only under tension, in this case provided by the object being retrieved. The knot is also relatively easy to tie and can be fashioned in any type of material.

TARBUCK KNOT (CARD 31)

Unfortunately for Tarbuck, his namesake knot became almost immediately redundant for its designated purpose thanks to the invention of kernmantel ropes, which could absorb sudden loads through their own elasticity, and which could be ruined by the untimely application of a Tarbuck Knot. However, the knot can still be utilized as a general slide and grip loop knot since, like the Prusik, it can be moved along by hand, and will lock under load. It is nowadays perhaps most widely used to pitch tents and to temporarily tether smaller boats in places where the tide will be going in or out. It is also extremely easy to untie.

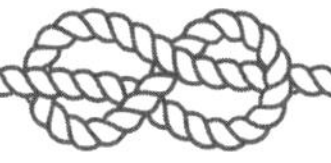

CHAPTER SIX

SPLICES

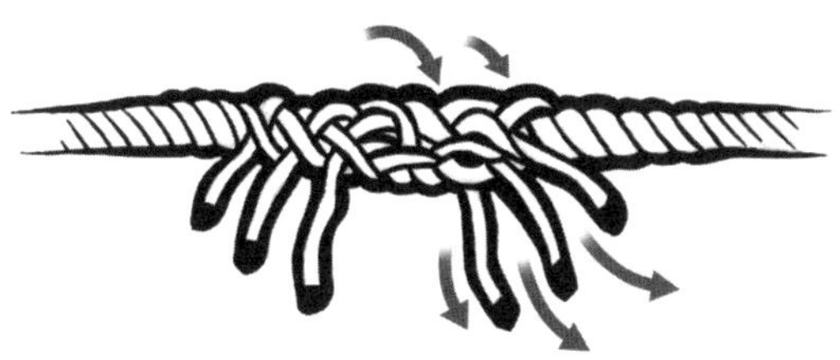

DEFINITION OF A SPLICE

A splice is a join made between two lines (usually ropes), or between two ends of the same rope, by unlacing the ropes' various threads and then weaving those threads together.

GENERAL PURPOSES AND USES

Rope splicing is most widely used at sea and has been for centuries. The practice is employed for three main reasons: to join ropes together in order to increase their length; to join the ends of one line to form a sling; and to repair a line which has been severed, snapped or otherwise worn through. Splices are also occasionally used to 'seal off' the end of a line and thus prevent it from fraying.

Splicing two lines together has the advantage of being more secure than simply knotting them – even the strongest knot decreases a given line's strength by 40%, while weaker knots can lessen a line's integrity even further. While not quite as strong as an unbroken line, a spliced rope retains up to 95% of its original strength, depending on which method is used. The only downside is that this usually results in a thickening of the line at the point where it is spliced, making it cumbersome to use under some circumstances.

CHARACTERISTICS OF A SPLICE

Simply put, splices require that the rope ends being joined have their strands unpicked to a pre-determined length before being

interwoven to join the two ropes – a completely different action to regular knotting that sets splices apart from bends. For obvious reasons, splicing can only be used on lines made of braided threads: three-strand rope is the most suitable, although the practice can be applied to ropes braided from 12 strands or even more. As already mentioned, splicing does have the often unwanted effect of thickening the line at the splicing point, although this can be reduced, if not completely eradicated, by tapering the strands to meld them more smoothly into the line.

Splices are semi-permanent. They can be unpicked if necessary, but this will damage the rope in question by splaying the formerly spliced strands, which will then need to be trimmed off.

Unlike other types of knot, splicing sometimes requires the use of particular tools, as not all rope lines are so easily unpicked; the marlinspike and fid can be especially helpful in unpicking and then splicing the strands of particularly new or stiff ropes

TYPES OF SPLICES

EYE SPLICE (CARD 32)

The Eye Splice is the best type of splicing to use with three-stranded rope, for which it is the most efficient way of forming a loop in the end of the line. The difference between the number of suggested tucks in earlier and later directions is down to a variation in materials used. With older, natural-fibre lines, three tucks would have been sufficient to make a strong splice, but more modern synthetic lines require the suggested five tucks before being strong enough to hold – although even more should be used if the line is to hold anything particularly heavy. While not especially difficult, this splice does require some care and practice to get right.

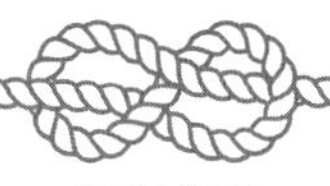

SHORT SPLICE (CARD 33)

The Short Splice can either be used to join two ends of the same piece of rope to form a sling or to meld together two entirely separate lines. It has various advantages, being relatively easy to learn, quick to carry out and consuming far less rope than other splices. As already noted, the Short Splice is also far stronger than any knot used for the same purpose, but the accompanying increase in diameter means that it cannot be used in any situation in which the line is expected to pass through a small eye or hole.

BACK SPLICE (CARD 34)

For many years, the Back Splice was most widely employed in the rope-making industry to finish off the end of a line and prevent any unwanted fraying or unravelling, although the prevalence of heat sealing in the production of modern synthetic lines – in which strands are simply melted and fused together – has largely rendered this practice obsolete.

The Back Splice does still have its uses, however. Like the Short Splice, it thickens the line used to make it, and when used to finish off the end of a rope this allows the end to be found by touch alone in situations where visibility is less than perfect. It is also quick and relatively easy to carry out, and as such is useful in emergencies or when time is otherwise of the essence.

CHAPTER SEVEN

STOPPER KNOTS

DEFINITION OF A STOPPER KNOT

A knot tied in a line either to prevent that line from unravelling or to stop it from passing through a small opening.

GENERAL PURPOSE AND USES

Stopper knots originated at sea, and remain widely employed in the rigging of sails today, although they can also be found in guy lines for the pitching of tents and in various creative pursuits such as macramé and Chinese rope design. The knots are also tied into the ends of multi-strand ropes to insure against unwanted fraying or unravelling – a purpose to which they are suited even when tied into thinner, more everyday lines such as thread, string and other household materials.

In addition, stopper knots can be used to create handholds or footholds in cases where ropes are being used for climbing purposes. Their suitability in these circumstances was first discovered aboard ships, where they were tied using the strands of unravelled rope (the rope then being rewoven above the knot) and used to ascend masts and rigging.

CHARACTERISTICS OF A STOPPER KNOT

The nature of their applications tends to demand stopper knots be fairly bulky, although their size does vary dramatically. Most are semi-permanent, strong and fairly stable, but can be easily untied, although some will seize up under strain and require cutting off, and others can be undone only when tied in a thicker cord or kept dry. The majority of stopper knots are tied in the end of a line, although there are certain exceptions to this rule that are tied in the bight.

Structurally, stopper knots can be divided into two categories: single-strand knots and multi-strand knots. Single-strand knots are those tied using just one piece of line, while multi-strand knots are those tied using the unpicked strands of lines usually composed of three or four strands; they become less effective when tied in lines made up of more strands than this.

TYPES OF STOPPER KNOTS

OVERHAND KNOT (CARD 34)

As well as being a stopper knot, the Overhand Knot is often used to make lines easier to grip by being tied at regular intervals to form a makeshift handrail; it is also occasionally used for purely decorative purposes. As a stopper knot, meanwhile, it is extremely versatile in terms of materials, capable of being tied into everything from thick rope to the thinnest of thread. That said, the simplicity of its structure belies its great strength: after being subjected to strain the knot can be virtually impossible to untie, especially in thinner lines or rope that has been exposed to water; the Double Overhand Knot, which adds a further pass to the original version, is even harder to unpick.

STEVEDORE'S KNOT (CARD 36)

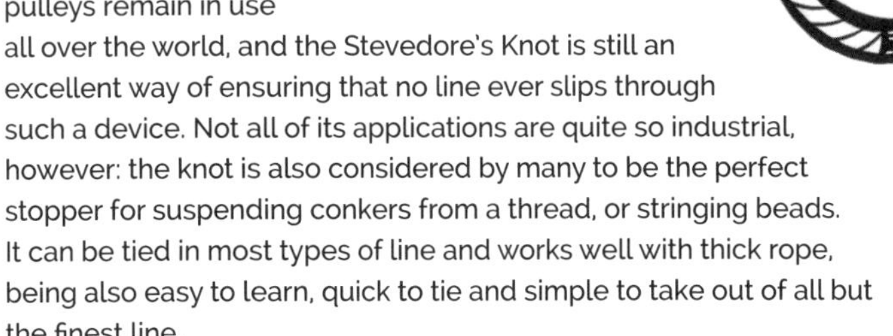

The loading and unloading of commercial cargo became automated long ago, although single rope pulleys remain in use all over the world, and the Stevedore's Knot is still an excellent way of ensuring that no line ever slips through such a device. Not all of its applications are quite so industrial, however: the knot is also considered by many to be the perfect stopper for suspending conkers from a thread, or stringing beads. It can be tied in most types of line and works well with thick rope, being also easy to learn, quick to tie and simple to take out of all but the finest line.

FIGURE OF EIGHT KNOT (CARD 37)

Like many stopper knots, the Figure of Eight Knot shares a degree of cross-pollination with knots from various other families, and can be easily altered to create a bend, hitch or loop. It is equally versatile in its role as a stopper knot, applicable in any situation in which a line needs to pass through a hole without running all the way through and escaping. As quick and simple to tie as it is to untie, the Figure of Eight is also fairly stable, although it is known to come undone if subjected to continuous oscillatory movements.

ASHLEY'S STOPPER KNOT (CARD 38)

The extremely bulky Ashley's Stopper Knot is generally used for all the same purposes as the popular Figure of Eight Knot, but takes precedence in instances where the Figure of

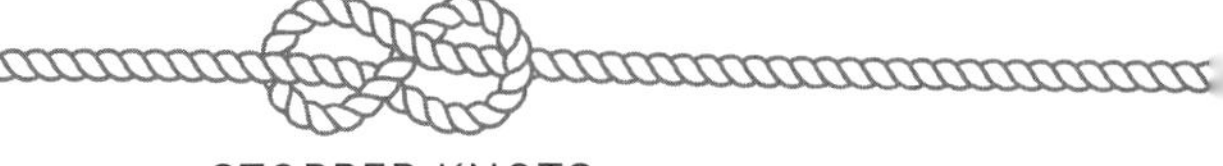

Eight is too small to prevent the line in question from escaping from whatever hole it is passing through. As such, it has many applications in sailing, as well as in the practice of pitching tents. The Ashley's Stopper Knot is relatively easy to learn and simple to tie and untie, but its size makes it better suited to heavier lines and less practical for use with thinner materials.

CROWN KNOT (CARD 39)

The Crown Knot is highly decorative and often finds employment in various artistic pursuits, but is of little practical use in and of itself. It is, however, widely used as a basis for more complex ropework: as well as the Back Splice, it also provides the structural foundation for Sennits and other lanyard knots. Combined with its reverse, the Wall Knot, it becomes a component of the appropriately named Wall and Crown Knot. It is generally tied with unpicked strands of rope like a splice, and as such is most commonly tied in three-strand line, although it can be made in line with a higher number of strands. The knot is solid and stable, and is fairly easy to learn and quick to tie.

DIAMOND KNOT (CARD 40)

While mostly used for decorative purposes, the Diamond Knot can still function as a stopper knot. It is usually tied in the standing part of a line using the unpicked strands of a rope, which are then re-woven together when they emerge from the knot. It can be tied with three- or four-strand line, and can be somewhat tricky to master initially. Once tied, it is strong and fairly permanent.

CHAPTER EIGHT

TRICK & FANCY KNOTS

Knots can fall into the trick knot category for a variety of reasons. Some do so because they are tied in a particularly impressive manner or unusually quickly; others will unravel when pulled in one direction, but not another. Yet more unravel in a spectacular fashion when placed under strain, while some are 'problem-solving' knots – namely, knots that can be tied to provide a solution to a riddle or to meet a particular or unusual need. Some fit several of the above criteria. Fancy knots, meanwhile, are those either tied in an elaborate way or which look particularly impressive or decorative when completed. Several of the knots included here fall into both categories.

While it goes without saying that 'problem-solving' trick knots have practical applications, it is also interesting to note that several of the other knots – even those that are designed to unravel easily or which rely on similar shortcomings for their 'trick' status – also have their own unique uses in the real world. These uses cover the entire knotting spectrum, as the knots included in this section come from several of the categories already covered, such as hitches, bends, binding knots and loops.

The trick knots' various origins are as diverse as the knots themselves. Some were discovered by accident while new variations on basic knot structures were being devised. Others were being used for practical purposes when their suitability for entertainment purposes was noted as a secondary characteristic.

As with a great number of the knots covered in this book, many trick knots were developed by sailors of centuries past, who used them to while away spare time at sea, and it was onboard ships that many such knots found their uses – some practical, some decorative. Indeed, trick knots have even been uncovered in some of the world's

most prestigious archives: Clifford Ashley, for example, discovered some that had been recorded in ethnographic reports by the Smithsonian Institute in Washington.

It should come as no surprise to find that some of the knots in this section are harder to tie than others – many of the easier ones may also require considerable practice to master in their 'trick' form. Almost all can be tied with almost any type of material, although anything too thick or too thin may make trick demonstrations more difficult. The only exceptions are those tricks in which a heavy load is placed on the line once the knot has been tied. In these cases, only line that has been verified as strong enough for the purpose at hand should be used, and great care should always be taken to ensure the safety of whoever is demonstrating the trick, as well as any spectators.

TYPES OF TRICK/FANCY KNOTS

GRIEF KNOT (CARD 41)

The Grief Knot has many of the failings common to the Granny Knot, although in this case it is these same failings – namely, the ability to come undone under tension thanks to its being 'diagonally unbalanced' – that make it a successful trick knot. Unlike the Granny Knot, however, the Grief Knot unravels in a rather spectacular manner, with each line feeding back through the coils of the knot before coming loose. That said, the knot does also have a few practical uses that don't focus on it coming undone, such as holding very light or temporary structures in place (it is technically a binding knot). It can be told apart from the Granny Knot at a glance by the fact that its two ends protrude from the knot on opposite sides; in the Granny Knot, they emerge on the same side.

THIEF KNOT (CARD 42)

The Thief Knot qualifies as a trick knot in that it can be used to trick someone into thinking it is a Reef Knot, although under careful inspection the two can be told apart in the same way as the Grief and Granny Knot: in a Reef Knot, the ends emerge on opposite sides of the knot, while in a Thief Knot they emerge on the same side. It is structurally a binding knot, but is known to spill or jam, and as such is fairly useless for anything more strenuous than holding closed a cloth bag.

TOM FOOL'S KNOT (CARD 43)

In spite of the legend, the Tom Fool's Knot is far from inescapable – the Handcuff Knot is a far better knot with which to restrain someone – but its trick knot status is assured thanks to the speed and ease with which it can be tied. The Tom Fool's Knot is a loop knot, and can be used as the basis of the Sheepshank; indeed, one of its original uses may well have been to tether more docile farm animals, which would have found it significantly harder to escape than most humans would have done.

TURK'S HEAD (CARD 44)

Aboard ships, the Turk's Head had one important purpose: it was tied onto the upper middle of the wheel to make it obvious when the boat was being steered in a straight line. This practice, known as 'marking the king spoke', was extremely useful for a number of reasons; most notably, it allowed the person steering to judge direction even at night or in periods of poor visibility. The great bulk of the knot also meant that it could be easily found by hand, aiding steering even in severe storms or periods of virtual blindness.

The knot was also used for various other purposes, including as a grip on ladders and guard rails, for the sealing of bags and even to secure anklets and bracelets. As such, the knot qualifies as both a trick knot and a fancy knot, the latter status guaranteed by its highly decorative appearance, and these days it can still be found in many intricate jewellery designs.

From a trick point of view, the knot enthusiast can impress their audience with their vast knowledge of the numerous variations on the Turk's Head – which in fact constitutes an entire family of knots, rather than just one.

Even more impressive would be an understanding of the mathematical formulae employed to plan a Turk's Head in advance. Any Turk's Head knot is said to have a number of 'leads' – namely, the number of times the line crosses as it goes around whatever object it has been tied around. The knot will also have a number of 'bends' or 'bights' – in this case, the number of times the line crosses itself along that same object's long axis (Turk's Head knots always being tied around a cylindrical object). The formulae come into play when the knot is to be tied with multiple strands of line: the number of strands will always be the same as the largest common factor of the number of leads and the number of bends, and any audience is sure to be impressed by the demonstrator having worked these numbers out in advance.

It should also be noted that there are three varieties of Turk's Head – another fact that can be used to wow an audience. The knots are said to be 'narrow' when there are two or more fewer leads than there are bends, 'square' in cases where the number of leads or bends is one greater than the other, or 'wide' when there are two or more fewer bends than leads. It is not possible to tie a Turk's Head with an equal number of bends and leads.

SHEEPSHANK KNOT (CARD 45)

For practical purposes, the Sheepshank is useful for shortening a line – for example, if the user wishes to remove undue strain from any part of a rope or cord that he or she thinks may have been damaged by past wear. There are several ways of tying a Sheepshank, and the method described here is the 'trick' version, qualifying as such thanks to the way in which tying it consists of fluid, seemingly simultaneous movements of previously prepared loops in the line.

SLIPPERY HITCH (CARD 46)

The trickery inherent in the Slippery Hitch stems from the fact that it is stable when weight is applied to one end, but comes undone when the other is pulled. In relation to the above riddle, therefore, this means that it can be used to get down from the cliff in question and then pulled undone from the bottom, thus impressing onlookers (although, needless to say, a cliff with an anchoring tree is not necessary for the demonstration – a smaller and preferably safer setup will suffice). Practically speaking, the Slippery Hitch has a few other uses: it can be employed to tether small, light boats (which leads to it being occasionally known as the Canoe Hitch), while the fact that it can be so easily released leads some to use it for securing sails to small sailboats.

MONKEY'S FIST (CARD 47)

The Monkey's Fist's original use has been well documented but, although weighing down a line may once have been a matter of life and death, these days it is more likely to be part of a performance trick. That said, the act of making a Monkey's Fist alone is something of an impressive feat; while not difficult in itself, the end result does look rather spectacular.

A line with a Monkey's Fist tied into it is also surprisingly useful in all sorts of unusual situations. Extreme climbers have been known to use them to help get single ropes over unusual rock formations before ascending them. In a more purely aesthetic application, the Maori people of New Zealand use the knot in the practice Poi, a type of juggling with balls attached to the ends of short ropes; originally used to develop strength and dexterity, Poi is now a ritualistic tradition amongst modern Maori tribes.

In addition to these uses, the Monkey's Fist can also be used purely for decoration. It is often found suspended from necklaces, key rings, earrings, cufflinks and the like, thus also qualifying it as a fancy knot. In the US, it has been adopted by the homeless community as a symbol of brotherhood and solidarity, and some homeless charities raise money by selling pieces of jewellery depicting the Monkey's Fist, many of them hand-crafted by homeless people themselves.

BOTTLE SLING (CARD 48)

The Bottle Sling is a trick knot for several reasons. Firstly, as Ashley proved, when tied properly it is so secure that it can be used to safely whirl a bottle around at height. Secondly, the mere act of tying it demands a certain level of dexterity – particularly in finishing the knot off properly. Finally, its ability to hold fast bottles, pitchers and jars can be especially pleasing to a captive audience – not least when those bottles are filled with beverages and then slung over the side of a small boat for cooling in the water below.

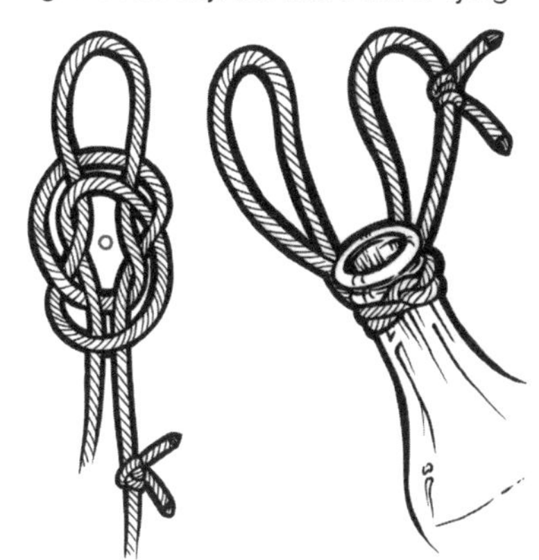

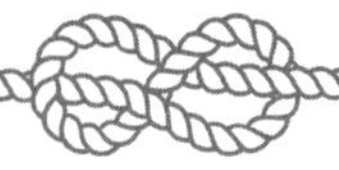

GLOSSARY

ANTICLOCKWISE LOOP A loop made by leading the working end in the direction against that taken by a clock's hands. Can be either underhand or overhand. See also Loop, Clockwise Loop, Overhand Loop and Underhand Loop.

BIGHT - A section of rope, between the working and standing ends, bent to create a curve or 'bump' in the line.

BRAIDING - Interweaving several strands of rope to create a pattern. Sometimes referred to as 'plaiting'.

BREAKING STRAIN/ STRENGTH - The average load under which a new, never-before-used rope will break, as calculated by the rope's manufacturer.

CABLE - A name generally used for any large rope, although the strict definition deems a cable to be a rope made up of three hawsers laid up together.

CAPSIZE - What happens to a knot when it becomes misshapen, usually from having too much weight placed upon it or not being adequately tightened.

CLOCKWISE LOOP - A loop made by leading the working end in the direction following that of a clock's hands. Can be either underhand or overhand. See also Loop, Anticlockwise Loop, Overhand Loop and Underhand Loop.

CORD - A line made up of several strands of yarn plaited together. In general, this name is applied to lines of diameter under 10mm (4 in) only.

DRAWLOOP - A loop that can be altered in size by pulling on the working end of a line.

EFFICIENCY - Official measure of a knot's strength. This is expressed as a percentage of the breaking strength of the rope.

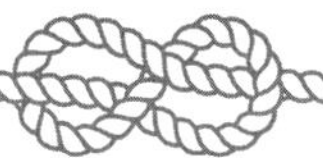

EYE - A small loop formed in the end of a rope. Also sometimes used as a name for a ring or hole through which line can be threaded.

FIBRE - The basic component of a natural-fibre rope.

FID - A small, pointed pin made of wood, used to assist with the loosening of rope strands.

FRAYING - Denotes wear in a rope wherein the rope's separate strands have begun to unravel.

HAWSERS - Large, three-stranded ropes of diameter larger than 10mm (4 in). Generally used for towing or mooring.

LANYARD - A short length of line used to tie down objects. Often decorated with knots.

LEAD - The direction the working end of a line takes as it goes through a knot, or the action of taking it through the knot.

LINE - A generic name for a rope, cable or similar. In strictly definitive terms, a line is a rope that has been used for a particular purpose – a clothes line, for example.

LOAD - To place weight on a knot or line. Also the weight under which a knot or line has been placed.

LOCKING TUCK - The final, vital stage of making a particular knot in an instance when, if this step were omitted, the knot would come undone or capsize.

LOOP - A circle made in a rope by passing the working end either under or over the standing part. See also Anticlockwise Loop, Clockwise Loop, Overhand Loop and Underhand Loop.

MAKE FAST - To tie a line to an object.

MARLINESPIKE/ MARLINGSPIKE - A metal instrument with a pointed end used to separate rope strands.

OVERHAND LOOP - A loop created in a line by placing the working end over the standing part. Can be either clockwise or anticlockwise. See also Anticlockwise Loop, Clockwise Loop, Loop and Underhand Loop.

PLAITING - See Braiding.

REEVING - Passing a rope through an opening such as a hole.

ROUND TURN - A turn in which the working end of a line is passed all the way around a rail, bar or similar object, bringing it back alongside its standing part as it comes out of the turn. See also Turn.

SAFE WORKING LOAD - The average weight that a rope can take without breaking, taking into account the rope's age, its prior usage and the knots involved. This may be as low as 6 per cent of the manufacturer's previously stated breaking strength. See also Breaking Strength.

SLING - An unbroken circle of rope or similar material.

STANDING END/STANDING PART - The section or end of a line not actively being used in creating a knot. See also Working End.

STRAND - A component of rope, made from twisting yarn together.

TUCK - The act of passing the working end of a line either through a loop or under the standing part to hold it in place.

TURN - One pass of a line around a rail, bar or similar object.

UNDERHAND LOOP - A loop created in a line by placing the working end under the standing part. See also Anticlockwise Loop, Clockwise Loop, Loop and Overhand Loop.

WHIPPING - The process of wrapping string or similarly narrow line around the end of a rope to prevent it from fraying.

WORKING END - The end of a line actively being used to create a knot. See also Standing End/Standing Part.

YARN - A line created by twisting together fibres. Yarn is then further plaited to create line with a larger diameter.